WAR
OF
2012

MAIN STREET VERSUS WALL STREET

Terol

AuthorHouse™
1663 Liberty Drive
Bloomington, IN 47403
www.authorhouse.com
Phone: 1-800-839-8640

© 2012 by Terol. All rights reserved.

No part of this book may be reproduced, stored in a retrieval system, or transmitted by any means without the written permission of the author.

Published by AuthorHouse   06/05/2012

ISBN: 978-1-4685-9904-6 (sc)
ISBN: 978-1-4772-0139-8 (hc)
ISBN: 978-1-4772-0138-1 (e)

Library of Congress Control Number: 2012908485

Any people depicted in stock imagery provided by Thinkstock are models, and such images are being used for illustrative purposes only.
Certain stock imagery © Thinkstock.

This book is printed on acid-free paper.

Because of the dynamic nature of the Internet, any web addresses or links contained in this book may have changed since publication and may no longer be valid. The views expressed in this work are solely those of the author and do not necessarily reflect the views of the publisher, and the publisher hereby disclaims any responsibility for them.

CONTENTS

The Affirmation 1
Corporate America 7
The New Generation Of Corporations 11
The Private Sector 26
Private Co-Ops 28
Our Town 30
Corporate America 2012 36
Health Care 45
The Nixon Doctrine 54
Candidate Obama 58
President Obama 61
The 21st Century 65
Right To Work Laws 68
The Minimum Wage 72
Main Street U.S.A. 76
The Reason 77
An Energy Plan 79
Issues 80
The American WORKER 85

Class Warfare 87
The War 91
The War Of 2012 99
About The Author 101

"The war of 2012" begins with a number of simple demands and will end at which time, those demands are met.

THE AFFIRMATION

America, the name itself extols the virtues of a nation dually endowed with all the natural resources, the ingenuity and innovation that never ceases to challenge the mind, along with the power and greatness to inspire and lift up a world, and become its leader. We are America the Beautiful, the land of the free and God has blessed us with un-ending opportunity and grace.

The American people can lay down their heads upon their pillows at night and know that they are protected by the most powerful military in the world, the most generous "harvest" the earth can yield, and an economy that has no limitations and freedoms enjoyed by no other peoples on earth.

America's greatness can only be hindered by its people and its government or by greed that overcomes the morals and values depicted by our "Constitution" and "Declaration of Independence".

America's true greatness must lie ahead as we seek to insure that the 21st century will end with the United States of America achieving all the goals that our founding fathers sat forth for us in 1776.

America is well over 200 years old and yet we are still in our infancy as we seek to achieve those goals given to us in 1776. We must take heart in the fact that our real future lies ahead and if we are to achieve our goals, we must first undo the failings of the 20th century, and insure that we never repeat the failings of the first 10 years of the 21st century.

In 2012 we must not dwell on the misgivings of the past, however we must understand how the greatest nation on earth took some missteps and ventured off the beaten path.

In the 20th century we talked about equal rights for all Americans, something guaranteed every American in "The Declaration of Independence" yet congress had to pass a law guaranteeing a woman the right to vote or to grant a black person the same rights enjoyed by white people.

In the 21st century we still have politicians telling stories of how their father or grandfather came to this country from a foreign land and realized the American dream, yet in the same speech they want to shut down the border between the U.S. and Mexico and deny the Mexican people, whose relatives lived on American soil long before Lewis and Clark blazed a trail westward, to work or live on American soil.

In 2012 and going forward perhaps we can protect our borders in a fair and humane way and have an immigration policy which unites North America and creates a bonding process that would allow the United States, Canada and Mexico to share their cultures and resources. In a world that now features a global economy, why was it that there's never been a North American economy?, an economy in which we could share natural resources, innovation and prosperity. The 10 Commandments say "love thy neighbor", really that could have a rather broad meaning.

In the 21st century in order to reach the goals of 1776 perhaps we need to re-define the phrase equal rights to mean that we will begin a bonding process that truly depicts the meaning and spirit of what our founding fathers believed to be equal rights under the law and under God.

In the 21st century the American people must tear down the barriers that have divided us both in this country and around the world in order for this great country to move ahead. The social, economic and political barriers are strictly ideological restraints on a country without boundaries.

In 2012 there must be war that frees us as a nation against those restraints that might stop us from reaching our goals sat forth for the 21st century and beyond.

The ideological restraints put on this country by politicians gone awry must be removed as we must seek the truth and eliminate the myths going forward.

This nation must rid itself of divisive politics and social anger that makes it impossible to come together and resolve the difficult problems that we will have to face in order to create a better nation for future generations.

The people must come together as one and forget about the issues that divide us and remember what we have to overcome in order to reach our goals of building a better nation for all our peoples.

The myth in the country that we were all created equal with equal opportunity for all must be seen for what it is and realize that the disparity of wealth and opportunity grew rapidly in the 20th century and has grown even more in the first 10 years of the 21st century.

The lack of opportunity for the poor and minorities played itself out in the 20th century and left 35 million people living in poverty, already in the 21st century that number has risen to 50 million.

In 2012 another 94 million people are seeing their rights and opportunities diminish as they linger ever so close to the poverty line as wages remain stagnant and jobs become harder to find. There's no equality for people living in poverty, minorities and the poor have known this for centuries, and now 40% of "the middle class" is now facing that prospect.

The prospects of having your freedom taken away is mind blowing to any American who in the past could buy a new home or a new car or adult toys or buy all the clothes that they wanted or eat in any restaurant as many times as they wanted.

It's not only about the equal rights and freedom guaranteed in "the Declaration of Independence" but it's also about the rights and freedoms taken from you when you fall into poverty and can't have the things that "middle class" Americans now have.

The wealthy in this country can't comprehend what it's like not to be able to enjoy the freedom that comes with wealth and power. A person can have all the rights in the world, but it does them no good if they don't have enough wealth to purchase the things they would like to have or need.

Opportunity has gone by the wayside for 50 million people in this country and for another 94 million people the window is closing and the myth is that there's nothing our government can do about it.

The truth is there are things the government can do to help out on main street U.S.A. and turn around an economy on "main street" that's strangling the poor and "the middle class", it's called investing in the American people and the country we love.

For the past 4 decades politicians have been intrigued by "corporate America" and what "corporate America" has to offer and forgotten about the fact that while "Wall Street" has prospered, "main street" has paid the price. Politicians have become the tool used by "Wall Street" to strip the American people of their wealth and their well being as they have been able to remove trillions of dollars from the consumer on "main street U.S.A."

The government must reign in "Wall Street" and give back the money taken from "main street" by "corporate America" and its entity's over the past 4 decades. "Corporate America" changed the business landscape in America and as a result the American people have paid a huge price and received nothing in return.

America is wealthier than its ever been as a result of its ability to export goods in a global economy that's growing by the minute and offering all the opportunity needed for "corporate America" and "Wall Street" to enjoy huge profits. "Corporate America" and

"Wall Street" are flush with cash while "main street" Americans are without jobs, underwater in their homes and trying to pay today's bills with the same income they earned in 1980.

Members of Congress will be campaigning for re-election in 2012 along with President Obama and perhaps they need to explain to the American people why they can't invest on "main street" when their cronies on "Wall Street" have trillions of dollars to invest in the global economy.

The American people in 2012 have the right to know if their elected officials will stand up for "main street" in the coming years or continue their "love affair" with "corporate America" and "Wall Street" and ignore the needs of the poor and the "middle class."

"The war of 2012" is about saving the "middle class" from the clutches of poverty and lifting the poor from the black hole that surrounds them and rebuilding a work force in America that's been decimated by "corporate America" and devious politicians.

CORPORATE AMERICA

We are "corporate America" the land of corporations and the home of the CEO's, as goes "corporate America" as goes the United States of America. Since the "corporate" take-over of America in the 1970's the American people have been held hostage by corporations and "Wall Street".

"Corporate America" feeds us, and furnishes us with our transportation, at a price of course. "Corporate America" manufactures our clothing, our furniture, overseas of course as well as builds our homes and finances them as well. "Corporate America" gives us our entertainment, electricity, energy and our politics, there's nothing that "corporate America" doesn't do for us, at a price of course. "Corporate America" is there for us when we come into the world, takes care of our health care needs while we are living and when we die, "corporate America" buries us.

Thank God for "corporate America"!!

"Corporate America" has given us everything we have today, including our political system, our economy and of course "Wall Street". In 2012 "corporate America" will give us a president and a new congress to which we will be truly grateful, after all we the American people aren't capable of electing the people who represent us.

"Corporate America" and the 200 CEO's that run the country are very pleased with the country they have created and the wealth that they have procured for themselves. They are extremely proud of the 435 individuals that they have hand picked to be in Congress and the special person they chose to be President. "Corporate America" is especially proud that they have been able to branch out and be able to hand pick over 30 governors in the country and they feel it won't be long before they are able to control all fifty states.

"Corporate America" is pleased that it was able to convince President George W. Bush to go to war in Afghanistan and Iraq so that the defense contractors in the country could have 10 great years to solidify their financial positions and stock price on "Wall Street".

"Corporate America" was truly grateful for the bailout it received from George W. Bush and members of Congress when all the major financial institutions were going bankrupt, it would have been a huge blow for the wealthy in the country had those banks failed and "corporate America" had lost its opportunity to borrow all that cheap money.

"Corporate America" was honored when President Obama took pity on a totally dysfunctional auto industry and bailed them out of bankruptcy before they could be procured by a foreign auto maker. U.S. auto makers have struggled since they were forced to build smaller cars, they have never been able to build a quality car for a reasonable price and make a profit, and perhaps they never will.

"Corporate America" wants to thank all the Presidents that have bailed out their "corporate" run airline industry, "corporate America" is more than grateful for the fact that they can use the bankruptcy system over and over again and never have to go out of business. "Corporate America" doesn't have to worry about making real profits on running a business the way a business should be run, they have the bankruptcy laws to protect them.

"Corporate America" wants to thank the American people for buying all of its cheap products that they make in foreign countries and sell in America. "Corporate America" is appreciative that the American people are not upset with them for creating jobs overseas and not in America.

"Corporate America" wants to say it's sorry that 50 million people are living in poverty in America and that another 88 million are living paycheck to paycheck but after all, "corporate America" does have to look out for "corporate America".

"Corporate America" represents the biggest threat to the American people in the 21st century and needs to be dealt with in a very serious way. When a handful of CEO's can greatly influence our economy, foreign affairs and our government itself, it's time for grave concern.

We the people have lost control of our country and our government and need to commit ourselves into rebuilding our communities from scratch and re-create the country we once knew when we created this country one community at a time.

It's not to late to return the country to the "capitalist" system we once knew and it's not to late to change every face in Washington, D.C. and restore our political system back to where our founding fathers intended it to be, representing the American people.

As long as "corporate America" has total control over "the United States of America" we the people will continue to be merely the servants of the 1% in a nation going nowhere.

THE NEW GENERATION OF CORPORATIONS

Entrepreneurs and "capitalism" was once the face of American business. Entrepreneurs and the spirit of "capitalism" once reigned supreme on the streets of "main street U.S.A.". Millions of small businesses across the nation were owned and operated by self motivated individuals with a plan in mind and a dream to fulfill.

This was the America that people talk about in 2012, but haven't seen for decades. This was the 1950's and 60's when an individual with $20,000 and a dream could fulfill a dream. America was growing rapidly in the 1950's and 60's as a population explosion was abound and the frontier spirit had grasped many Americans. President Eisenhower was creating a national highway system and Americans went on the move.

Entrepreneurs were coming out of the woodwork and the U.S. economy was booming. Entrepreneurs are gamblers at heart and new opportunities for opening a business was to never be better. The sun belt states were being seen as a great new place to raise a family and the move was on. Wherever there's population growth and "capitalism" the number of businesses will grow as well and the number of entrepreneurs needed to own and operate those businesses accelerated rapidly. Much like the Gold Rush in 1849 the great American boom was on and an opportunity was to be found all over America for that gambler with $20,000.00 in his pocket.

Millions of entrepreneurs did come out of the woodwork in the 1950's and 60's and did create tens of millions of start-ups in order to satisfy the needs of that growing population. Entrepreneurs had now become a major player in the lives of the American people. They were supplying the people on "main street U.S.A." With the goods and services they needed as well as supplying the jobs that would allow these new communities to survive and prosper.

These new business owners were on top of their game as most businesses were prospering and their owners were becoming the pillars of their communities and the heyday of the American entrepreneur and "capitalism" had arrived. The local business owner was looked upon as a leader and the one who would be the steward of the community and protect the community and its economy. The business owners provided the income for the community as they were the job creators and the distributor of the wealth in their community.

It was the entrepreneur in the neighborhood who would provide the leadership and direction for the local government and it was their leadership and success that would determine the conviction of the local economy. A city, town or community was dependent upon the abilities and imagination of it entrepreneurs and whether those communities grew or not was dependent upon the relationship between the people and the business sector.

Entrepreneurs in this country had found their mojo in the 1950's and 60's and nearly every local economy was thriving and growing and this was the perfect scenario for the U.S. Economy to become the strongest and wealthiest in the world. By 1970 entrepreneurs and small business owners, had created the greatest economy the world would ever see and the United States and it's people were definitely on a "sugar high".

The American businessman was enjoying life in the 1950's and 60's, everything seemed to be going their way. A growing population had allowed them the opportunity to start-up a business and the wealth and jobs that they provided the community had enabled those communities to grow, creating more wealth.

"Capitalism" was working on "main street U.S.A." in the 1950's and 60's and all the cities, towns, and communities were growing and thriving. "Capitalism" was working because, American entrepreneurs in the 1950's and 60's abided by and respected "the capitalist system" of government.

> ## "Capitalism"
>
> 1. An economic system, characterized by open competition in a free market, in which the means of production and distribution are privately or corporately owned and development is proportionate to increasing accumulation and reinvestment of profits.
>
> 2. A political or social system regarded as being based on capitalism.
>
> American Heritage Dictionary

In the 1950's and 60's there was open competition in a free market in the United States of America and this is what allowed an individual with $20,000.00 and a plan to own a business and be successful on "main street U.S.A." In the 1950's and 60's nearly all the businesses on "main street U.S.A." were owned and operated by a small businessman who started his business with $20,000.00 and a plan and who was now successful and profitable. Open competition can mean many things to many people, but to the small businessman on "main street U.S.A." in the 1950's and 60's it meant that producing a quality product and good service was the key to success and that's what they did.

In the 1950's and 60's the small businessman knew that in order to keep their economy strong locally that they needed to support their local economy and that's what they did, they supported their local economy. The small businessman distributed the revenues of his business back into his own community.

The small businessman distributed the revenues of his business back into his local community by buying his supplies locally and using the local repairman to fix his equipment. The small businessman had first invested in his community by having a local builder build his building and local painters to paint the building. The small business owner had already purchased the equipment and fixtures for his business locally and also had chosen a local accountant and attorney to handle his accounting and legal affairs. Entrepreneurs in the 1950's and 60's first invested their own money in their local communities and then distributed the revenues of that business back into the local community.

The American businessman in the 1950's and 60's invested heavily into his community when he started up his business and he would continue to invest in his community when he distributed the revenues from that business back into the local economy while he did business in the local community.

The American entrepreneur in the 1950's and 60's understood that community was everything and keeping that community growing was pertinent in the success of their business and a true gauge in whether the economy in a local community is growing or not is, what's the median income? This median income and population of a community depicts the buying power of a community and no business owner wants to see the buying power of the community he does business in diminish.

The American entrepreneur knew lots of things in the 1950's and keeping the median income in his community up was one of those things and he knew the only way to do that was by increasing population or wages and that he could control wages.

Being self employed usually means you have a number of employees and in the 1950's and 60's you wanted a special kind of employee, one that would make you money and you were comfortable with. In the 1950's and 60's service was utmost in most businesses and having the best employees generally meant you gave the best service and had the best chance to be successful. Back when we strived for quality and service, not speed and price, so we wanted the best employees we could get.

Entrepreneurs back when, knew that the cost of training a good employee could be very high, so when we hired someone we wanted them to be the best person available, and if they were, it would be up to us to keep them for a long period of time. For many of us when we hired an employee we never expected them to leave and we did everything we could to see that they stayed. The two biggest concerns for an employee are working conditions and a decent pay package that they can live on and we tried to provide both.

Providing a safe, efficient and pleasant work place for our employees was a number one priority for a number of reasons. A safe work place was pertinent because no one wanted to be subjected to unnecessary dangers while on the job and no one wanted to see an employee get hurt. Workers compensation and other insurances would go up dramatically if there was an accident of any kind. The third reason for providing a safe work place was good employees were not likely to work in a job they considered dangerous.

In order to keep good help small business owners would have to be fair with their employees and treat them with dignity and respect. We worked with our employees side by side and hand in hand, we were on the premises directing traffic, hands on management and our employees became like family, we spent far more time with our employees than we did with our family. Dissension didn't work well in the work place in the 1950's and 60's so as an employer there was a fine line to walk when we dealt with our employees, and the employer who did it best had the best employees.

Way back when, employers were at the mercy of their employees because it was those employees that would be responsible for the quality of that product you were producing as well as the demeanor in which that product was served or presented. Quality and service once meant something in this country and the business that produced the highest quality product or provided the finest service would always win out. We did not accept absentee ownership as a way of doing business in the 1950's and 60's and we knew if we did our business would fail because the "people" wanted and expected the highest quality product and the best service that their money could buy.

Working conditions was a number one priority for workers in the 1950's and 60's, however the American worker back then also expected "a living wage" and a decent pay package. The pay package had to include a health insurance plan that covered everything and had no deductible and covered everyone in their family. The pay package must also include paid vacation, overtime pay and sick leave, most employees would also expect a nice Christmas bonus and some week-ends off. A good employee would get all of the above plus the dignity and respect that they felt they deserved plus a little praise from time to time from their boss.

Organized labor had gained a foot hold on "main street U.S.A. and most employees were or would be union members, small businesses in the 1950's and 60's were rapidly teaming with organized labor and together were providing for an American work force that could provide a comfortable lifestyle for their employees. In the 1950's and 60's businesses that didn't unionize usually paid their employees the equivalent of that paid a union worker doing the same job or in some cases even more, workers in the 1950's and 60's were a valuable piece of the business landscape in America and were treated appropriately.

Entrepreneurs in the 1950's and 60's understood their responsibilities to themselves, their family, their employees, their communities and their country and they understood what they had to do to fulfill those obligations. We understood as business owners if we failed, we put our family in jeopardy, our employees and their families in jeopardy and the money that we were generating would now be lost to our community as well not to mention the money that could have been distributed and reinvested in our local neighborhood for years to come. We knew that our community depended upon us for our financial assistance and leadership and to fail could be catastrophic.

The 1950' and 60's was a time for exuberance in the business world as things couldn't have been better, most businesses were profitable beyond expectations, our employees were being well paid and enjoying an exceptional lifestyle and our communities were growing and prospering thanks to an ever increasing tax base. As business owners we knew that we're doing our share by generating the income that allowed our local economy to grow and prosper and that our physical involvements and decision making would allow our communities to grow and prosper for years to come and in turn do our small part in making the main street U.S.A. economy strong and the U.S. economy the strongest in the world.

In 1960 in a smoke filled room a small group of union leaders were getting together in an effort to draw up a plan to help John F. Kennedy defeat Richard M. Nixon in the 1960 election for president of the United States. These union leaders would take occasional breaks and the conversation would turn to economic issues and during one of those conversations 5 of these individuals began discussing what the business landscape in America would look like in the year 2000, and out of nowhere would come this strange prediction.

Those 5 union leaders predicted that by the turn of the century that big business would own and operate nearly every business in America and that organized labor would struggle to maintain their share of the work force in America. This prediction was made at a time when 85% of all the jobs in America was either created by the government or small privately owned businesses, owner operated.

Would the prediction made by those 5 union leaders in that smoked fill room in 1960 come true?, or would small privately owned businesses continue to grow and prosper?

The 1970's would prove to be the beginning of the end of "capitalism", the entrepreneur, and the individual who just wanted to own and operate a business and have the outside chance of achieving the American dream. By 1970 the business landscape on "main street U.S.A." was beginning to change and "main street" was taking on a new look. A new generation of corporations were beginning to invade our local communities in a big way and the way we used to do business on "main street U.S.A." was about to change.

The American people were beginning to eye an all new way of eating, it was called fast and cheap, and it was catching on. For nearly 200 years America had been about quality and service and now it was about fast and cheap. Fast food outlets run by a number of corporations were popping up all over the place and restaurant owners around the country were seeing a new competitor that would pack a punch. This was not a traditional competitor that competed in a traditional way, this competitor was not a business run and operated by a small entrepreneur trying to support his family, this competitor was a billion dollar corporation who didn't care about quality and service, but relished speed and a low price. Business on "main street" was changing and the American entrepreneur was about to run out of luck.

The fast food industry not only changed the way America ate, but it did something far more telling, it changed the way we do business. No longer is business about quality and service or made in the U.S.A., it's now about fast and cheap and who cares where it's made. The fast food industry proved to every CEO in America that the American people would purchase products short on quality if the price was right and the labels like "union made" or "made in the U.S.A." had little meaning.

Fast food outlets would spring up all over America creating millions of jobs and making corporate franchises the darling of the business world. Several corporations had been selling fast food franchises for decades, however those franchise totals would go up 10 fold in the 1970's.

The fast food business was booming as Americans fell in love with their favorite fast food franchise, and sales were skyrocketing. However those sales had to come from somewhere, and that somewhere was from all the small privately owned restaurants in America. Every time a new franchise store would open a small businessman would close his doors and go out of business. This tit for tat might not have been seen as such a bad thing in America but looking back we now know better.

Lots of things would happen when a fast food franchise would open and a small privately owned restaurant would close their doors and go out of business. Number 1; the fast food franchise would hire 40 employees and pay them "a non living wage" with no benefits, when the small privately owned restaurant would go out of business, 40 employees earning "a living wage" with benefits would lose their jobs and the local union would lose 40 members.

Number 2; the local community would lose 40 people who counted on their jobs to pay their house and car payments and to raise their family. These were people who were valuable pieces in the community who earned good wages and paid their share of taxes and now in turn the community gets 40 kids trying to earn a few dollars to buy a car.

Number 3; Every time a community loses a good union job and that job is replaced with a minimum wage job, that community loses tens of thousands of dollars in a matter of a year and over decades, millions of dollars.

Number 4; The fast food industry figured out how to do something that big business and corporations hadn't been able to, keep the unions on the sidelines. The fast food industry had grown so fast and made so much money that the unions couldn't get through to their employees.

Organized labor made a huge mistake in their decisions regarding the fast food industry, mainly because they felt it would be a tough fight and getting "minimum wage" employees might not be worth it, but in the long run retailers, home improvement stores and big box stores would follow suit leaving 40 million American workers defenseless against "corporate American".

Number five; This new generation of corporations which include the fast food industry, big box stores, home improvement centers and retail stores not only replaced businesses that employed union workers and destroyed wage scales across American but they violated every rule of a "capitalist" society. "The new generation of corporations" did not do business with other businesses in a community, they did not distribute income in the community and they did not reinvest any of the money they made in the community back into that community, like the entrepreneurs had done in prior decades.

Number six; In order to make their scam work on the American people "the new generation of corporations" first had to skirt the unions which they did and then they had to find products cheap enough to sell at a low price and the fast food industry was able to do that, and thanks to the American people, mediocre food served warm or heated worked for them.

By 1980 the fast food industry had expanded nationwide into every American city, town and neighborhood and for every fast food franchise that opened, that city, town or community would lose over a million dollars a year in total revenue. This was not to be the largest hit these communities would take however, during the 1970's and 80's another sector of the "main street" economy was about to be destroyed as well, as big box stores were being built.

The "main street" economy and organized labor had taken a huge blow when fast food outlets invaded the streets of America and began to destroy the wage scale of the American worker, but the worst was still to come, "the big box stores". No one could have imagined the damage that "the big box stores" was about to do to the "main street" economy.

"Big box stores" would use the same business model created by the fast food industry, cheap products and low prices and knowing that the fast food industry had been able to defy organized labor, they understood that they didn't have to pay their employees "a union wage". Knowing that they could pay their employees the "minimum wage" now all the "scabs" had to do was find cheap products to sell and it didn't take them long.

The big box stores knew that union made products made in America would not give them the edge they needed to undercut the retail stores doing business at the time price wise, so they came up with a plan and the rest is history, they would buy or manufacture their products overseas, where sweat shops would enable them to produce products at half the cost.

The fast food industry have already began the process that would eventually destroy the "main street" economy and now "the big box stores" has come with the plan that would finish off the "main street" economy.

When "big box stores" began buying their products overseas small manufacturing plants around the country began to feel the pinch and when "the big box stores" began to have their products manufactured overseas those manufacturing plants began to close down. Millions of good paying manufacturing jobs were lost forever in America, when thousands of small manufactures closed down because they couldn't compete in price with overseas imports.

"The big big box stores" over a thirty year period has cost the "main street" economy 20-30 million good paying jobs because they import their products and pay their employees "a non living wage" and these good paying jobs will not return.

In order to compete openly in a free market the retail sector of the economy had to follow suit and join "the big box stores" by importing their goods and products as well in the 1990's and this would mean nearly every clothing, furniture and garment manufacturer in the country would close down, causing huge financial hardships for many "main street communities.

Retail outlets would also have to adjust their pay scales in order to compete with "the big box stores" and for many working in retail it would mean working part time or for "a non living wage" and little in the way of benefits.

The discounters in this country, those who feel that selling a mediocre product with little or no service, have made it big in America and around the world, as they have done well in the global economy, however at what price to the American people.

The American people have paid a huge price by ignoring the damage done by these new generation of corporations that have destroyed our work force in this country and made trillions of dollars off the backs of the American worker.

THE PRIVATE SECTOR

Politicians love to throw around the words private sector or private enterprise when talking about the business landscape on "main street U.S.A.", their way of describing non governmental operations on 'main street U.S.A." is to say that all other businesses are members of the private sector.

There are millions of businessmen in this country that own or used to own businesses on "main street" that take exception to those comments as we have never considered "corporate America" as being part of the private sector or any corporate entity being part of the private sector.

"Private Enterprise"

1. Business activities unregulated by state ownership or control; privately owned business in general.

2. A privately owned business enterprise, esp., one operating under a system of free enterprise or laissez-faire "capitalism".

The American Heritage Dictionary

In the minds of the millions of entrepreneurs and the small business owners who did or does business on "main street U.S.A. and created the businesses that made America strong, we resent the fact that politicians include "corporate America" as being part of the private sector.

Entrepreneurs and small business owner have nearly become dinosaurs in the business world as no small business start-ups has much chance of surviving in the 21st century. The very idea of being self-employed in this country has become more like a nightmare than a dream because a small business can no longer compete with 'corporate America" on "main street U.S.A.".

"The private sector" only does about 15% of all the business on "main street U.S.A." any more, "Corporate America" and the new generation of corporations does the remaining 85%, so there's not much reason for members of congress or the president to talk much about the private sector and jobs in the private sector, unless they honestly would like to help rebuild the "real" "private sector".

The private sector in America has become irrelative, we can no longer produce good paying jobs for our neighbors, we no longer can support our local charities or clubs, we can no longer insure that our local government has the money they need to take care of their people, we no longer have businesses that create profit that we can reinvest back into our neighborhoods and we no longer have the ability to keep the money generated in our cities and towns, in our cities and towns.

PRIVATE CO-OPS

Politicians talk about "capitalism" and entrepreneurs and the American dream, the truth is they can talk about it, but they are not going to be able to provide those opportunities for those entrepreneurs to live the American dream until there's "capitalism" back on the streets of "main street U.S.A."

There are millions of young people in the country today who dream about owning their own business and creating the businesses of the future with all new products and services, the only obstacle in their way, they need to be able to do business on a level playing field with "corporate America." "Capitalism" is about open competition in a free market and unfortunately that doesn't exist on main street U.S.A. in 2012.

A self-employed person in 2012 has to compete with "corporate America" and it's entities which all have national name recognition, national advertising, a national architectural firm, a national legal and accounting firm, a national buying program and a universal credit line supplied by "Wall Street".

If it's so difficult for members of congress or the president to understand why it's nearly impossible for an entrepreneur to open up their first business on "main street" and succeed in 2012 perhaps they need to have some conversations with the millions of entrepreneurs who have tried to own a business on "main street U.S.A. and couldn't compete with "corporate America".

21st century entrepreneurs need a level playing field on which to compete with "corporate America" or other wise they will end up in bankruptcy, losing their family and with no future, much like the entrepreneurs who have lost their businesses in recent years due to "corporatism".

21st century entrepreneurs need the same national programs that corporate stores have in order to compete and that's what the small business administration should be about, creating a level playing field for the "real" private sector. If the S.B.A. should not be able to create a condition in America where new entrepreneurs could compete and be successful, there are millions of old entrepreneurs in this country, that could assist them in doing so.

21st century entrepreneurs need private co-ops to provide them with the same national network enjoyed by corporate entities, in order for them to be successful like the entrepreneurs in the 1950's, 60's, and 70's. If members of congress and the president are truthful when they say they want to see small privately owned businesses to be successful so "main street" then they must create the level playing that would make it possible.

The "dilemma" for those who believe in American business and "capitalism" is this; in order for "capitalism" to work there must be "open competition" in a "free market" and there cannot be "open competition" when there's not a level playing field.

OUR TOWN

There are tens of thousands of cities, towns and communities in this country and every one of them is important to and is part of the "main street" economy and in turn the U.S. economy, the U.S. economy is made up of all the local economies in this country and by its GDP. Every local economy plays a role in the success of the U.S. economy and when thousands of these small economies are not doing well the "main street" economy does not do well. Politicians in Washington D.C. can't understand why the stock market can do well and the GDP numbers can be up, but the "main street" economy is in the toilet, it's very simple, the stock market and GDP are not part of "main street" America.

Every city, town and community in America has their own economy and nearly every local economy on "main street" has been decimated by the lack of wealth and income. The median family income in most local economies has been falling or remaining stagnant for nearly 30 plus years or since the new generation of corporations became part of those communities. If the median family income in a community depicts a middle class income then that community can be judged to be "middle class" and when the median family income drops below that level the community can be described as being impoverished. The median family income is important to the status of any community.

Median family income in an area can be driven up or down by a number of scenario's, however the number one scenario is wages. When wages go up in a community the median family income goes up and when wages go down the median family income goes down, so what's happened in the past 30 plus years?

Every governor of a state, supervisor of a county or a mayor of a city should know that every time a fast food outlet or "a big box store" opens its doors in a community the median family income goes down, when any discounter opens its doors the median family income for that community goes down. Every time a business enters a state or a city or community that does not pay "a living wage" the median family income goes down. Any time a state enacts "a right to work law" the median family income in that state goes down. State governors have to know that the quickest way there is to create poverty is to enact "right to work laws".

Local communities around the country depend on the fact that the median family income in their community will increase each year in order to stabilize their tax base and their economy. The largest destabilizing factor in a community is when the population goes up and the median family income goes down or stays the same.

300 million Americans don't depend or count upon "Wall Street" or the Gross Domestic Product to provide for their well being, most Americans would not give a damn if "Wall Street"

crashed, most Americans just want to live in a community where they can work and provide for their families. Americans are all about where they live, work and play and if the local economy is good, to hell with the rest of the world.

Politicians in 2012 need not worry about the next war they want to start or the Dow Jones and "Wall Street", they need not worry about tax cuts for them and their wealthy friends, politicians need not to worry about "corporate America" and the new generation of corporations, politicians need not worry about the greedy bastards that have taken all the money away from "main street" and the American people, politicians need to worry about the tens of thousands of local communities on "main street U.S.A." that have no wealth and shrinking, revenues.

Politicians must know that "main street U.S.A." is in need of serious repair and that nearly every city, town community or state needs some kind of help and that the "main street" economy has to be re configured from the bottom up and it's not a national issue, it's a local issue.

The rebuilding of "main street U.S.A." will begin in it's local communities and with the leadership of city councils, mayors and governors who need to go back to the drawing board, and come up with real plans to solve real problems.

Local communities must come up with ways to keep the money earned in their cities or towns in their communities, they must remain conscience of businesses in their city that don't distribute revenue back into the city or won't reinvest their profits.

"Capitalism" can work for a local community if the businesses follow the rules.

Leaders in local communities must know that businesses that buy their products overseas and pay their employees a non living wage are not good for their communities. Mayors must know that without open competition and free markets entrepreneurs can't open new businesses and survive. Local leadership must provide a business landscape with a level playing field in order for new start-ups to be successful, this will not happen unless they are capable of looking outside the box and be creative.

In 2012 there needs to be a new way of doing business in America, "a working grid" that works for the American work force and the "American people, not "corporate America". In 2012 the help from Washington D.C. needs to go directly to the local communities in this country and not "corporate America".

"The new generation of corporations" created an economic free fall on the streets of America during the last half of the 20th century causing the middle class to shrink and poverty to rise. "Corporate America" changed their way of doing business in the 20th century by destroying "capitalism" and the ability of entrepreneurs to do business in this country.

The restaurant sector which had provided tens of millions of jobs that paid "a living wage" during the 1st 70 years of the 20th century and proved to be a valuable social outlet for every community in America, now has been reduced to an industry that still has tens of millions of employees, however the jobs are meaningless. Paying "a non living wage".

The manufacturing sector has lost millions of good paying jobs that won't come back due to the fact that the retail sector of the economy made a decision to buy their goods from foreign countries instead of the United States of America.

The corporate discounters in this country played on the whims of the American people who felt that cheap and fast was better than quality and good service, or that wearing clothes that shrink and fade was better than clothes with a label that said made in America.

The American people fell in love with "cheap and fast" and they learned how to assemble toys and furniture. They even learned how to buy their clothes one size bigger, so they would fit after being washed, the people even learned to ignore the fact that the labels on the goods they buy don't say "made in America", however there's one thing the American people can't ignore, there's 55 million Americans living in poverty and 22 million Americans un-employed.

The exuberance of the American people to eat at fast food restaurants and to buy products made overseas has played right into the hands of "corporate America" and has enabled "corporate America" to take trillions of dollars off "main street U.S.A." and give it to "Wall Street". For forty years "corporate America" has stripped the wealth from "main street U.S.A." and the American people have done nothing about it and "corporate America" will continue to take from the American people until the people say enoughs, enough.

"The new generation of corporations" have destroyed 40 plus million good paying jobs over the past 40 years because they refuse to pay "a living wage" and work with organized labor, over a third of the American work force now work in a meaningless job.

"The new generation of corporations" were totally responsible for shutting down clothing and furniture manufacturers in this country that cost millions of good paying jobs and placed hardships on hundreds of small communities in this country that housed these manufacturers. Many of these small communities are now impoverished and on the government dole.

"Main street U.S.A." and the thousands of cities, towns and communities that make up "main street U.S.A." must rebuild their economies from the ground up and that requires cash and the fastest way to get cash on "main street U.S.A." is by increasing "the minimum wage" and requiring "the new generation of corporations" that have defied organized labor to pay "a living wage".

Wages are to "main street" what GDP is to "Wall Street" and the huge disparity in wages in the country caused by "corporate greed" must be dealt with if "main street U.S.A. is to have an economic renaissance.

CORPORATE AMERICA 2012

"Corporate America" and the new generation of corporations will soon be paying the full price for what they have done to the self-employed and other entrepreneurs and to the "main street" economy. "Corporate America" and the new generation of corporations were entrusted by the American people to provide for the needs of the American people, and now as predicted by the entrepreneurs who used to care for the needs of the American people, have failed the American people.

"Corporate America" never cared about the American people, "corporate America" only cared about what the American people could produce for them and the profits they could make for them. "Corporate America" needs the American people when it comes to working in their stores and doing their dirty work and producing the income and working for "minimum wage".

"Corporate America" needs the American people to spend what money they have left buying up their cheap foreign made products so that they might be able to stay in business. "Corporate America" needs the American people when it comes to cheap labor or when it comes to buying their foreign made products, otherwise "corporate America" doesn't give a damn about the American people.

By 2012 however, "corporate America" has finally dug itself a hole deep enough that it won't be able to get out of. During the past 40 years "corporate America has not abided by the spirit of "capitalism", and this will prove to be their demise on "main street U.S.A."

"Corporate America" saw no need to re-invest their profits on "main street U.S.A.", they decided to re-invest their profits on "Wall Street" and in foreign country's. "Corporate America" never distributed its operating cash on "main street U.S.A." but in foreign country's and with foreign entity's instead. "Corporate America" never shared any of its cash with its employees or their family's. "Corporate America" just took every dollar they could off "main street U.S.A."

When "corporate America" decided to have their goods and merchandise manufactured overseas, thereby shutting down manufacturing plants on "main street U.S.A.", perhaps they forgot about the fact that they would someday need a strong economy on "main street U.S.A." in order to survive.

In the past 40 years "corporate America" has taken all the money from "main street U.S.A." cut all the wages paid on "main street U.S.A." and driven all their competition out of business on "main street U.S.A.", and now its just "corporate America" doing business on "main street U.S.A." where there's no money left.

"Corporate America" wanted to ruin the "capitalist" system in America and prove that "capitalism" should only work for the wealthy and they have accomplished their goal, however it's hard to envision a bright future for "corporate America" as they operate on "main street", because the economy on "main street" is 6 feet under.

"Corporate America" has dug its own grave when it comes to doing business in the United States of America and will have to rely on the global economy to survive. "Corporate America" has played a big role in the "main street" economy for over 50 years and now some of its entities are growing older and becoming more irrelevant.

The fast food industry has been around for more than 60 years and lots of things have changed on "main street" but most of those hamburgers and chicken sandwiches have remained the same. The fast food industry has struggled to come up with new ideas or innovations that might bring new life or energy to a business that's been around longer than most of its customers.

The fast food industry grew because it had that special niche that people liked and it was a cheap and quick way to enjoy a meal, however after 60 years that special appeal is wearing thin.

Corporate CEO's in the fast food industry will now be forced to earn their money because they can no longer expect their stores to earn a profit like they could in the 70's and 80's. The "main street" economy that the fast food industry helped to destroy is now coming back to haunt them. CEO's are having to face the fact that they have many stores that may be 30-50 years old and in need of repair and many are in marginal neighborhoods and tough decisions will have to be made as to closing stores or remodeling them or even rebuilding from scratch. Many stores may be in areas that have far to many fast food locations in relation to population, over-building has become a huge problem for the retail industry as well.

Over-building, an aging product, older buildings and a bad economy will cause many sleepless nights for CEO's in the fast food business and as these CEO's decide which businesses to close or remodel 100's of thousands of jobs will be on the line leading to higher un-employment figures for the U.S. economy.

Retail may take a bigger hit than the fast food industry in the coming years as they face many of the problems the fast food industry is facing as well as difficulties created by e-commerce. By the end of the decade the way retail purchases are made may be totally different than the way we do it today.

The future of the retail industry will be up in the air for many years to come as retail transitions from catalog to retail stores and mail order to on line sales. CEO's in the retail industry will be going places no one has ever gone before and will earn their money because they will be making their decisions based strictly on unknown factors and circumstances.

One can only assume that there will be many stores closing in the retail sector due to over-building and this transitional state of the industry, and one can predict with certainty that this will lead to huge job losses. In the coming years the "main street" economy could lose millions of new jobs as the fast food and retail industries try to re-invent themselves.

The airline industry will be another negative for jobs in this country going forward as bankruptcy and consolidation is never good for job growth. In an industry that has seemingly never shown a profit and has used the bankruptcy laws to stay in business, 2012 will be business as usual as the year will start out with a major bankruptcy by a major airline that will cause thousands of job losses and the elimination of a number of flights flown.

The airline industry has certainly been the victim of the aftermath of 9/11 and a poor economy as well as an oil industry run by OPEC and manipulated by Wall Street but the industry itself is a perfect example of how "corporate America" can't run anything successfully for any length of time. 2012 will be another year in which the airline industry rids itself of 10's of thousands of good playing jobs and places a bigger burden on the "main street economy".

The oil industry will actually add jobs in 2012 as they merge with and acquire a number of natural gas businesses and drastically increase the number of fracking operations in the country. Natural gas offers up the opportunity to create millions of good paying jobs in this country and the government should jump on the band wagon and support this growing industry. The natural gas business created many of the jobs in 2011 and will be one of the few industries to actually increase hiring in 2012.

The oil industry knows a winner when it sees one and it will be a major player in the natural gas business going forward, surprisingly the coal industry hasn't become more involved in "shale" as it seems as if the natural gas business would be more in line with the coal industry than it is with the oil industry.

In the next decade the energy business could become one of America's great exports and balance out what we import in oil and as the coal and natural gas industry's will export more and more of their resources overseas.

Along with the oil and natural gas industry the "corporate" run health care system will be the other sector that will increase hiring in 2012 and most of these jobs will pay well and come with benefits as an aging population will require more health care and rehabilitation and long term care centers will continue to generate jobs as they have in the past decade.

The "corporate" run health care system will continue to grow at least as long as its ability to increase prices and its continuing efforts to buy out any privately owned health care entity's exist. What lies in the future for "corporate" run health care is suspect, however for 2012 the system will continue to increase hiring, and generate billions in profits.

In 2012 the auto industry will contribute approximately the same amount of jobs that it did in 2011 as U.S. auto makers will sell about the same amount of cars as they did in 2011. Auto makers will sell more cars in the United States in 2012 but will sell less vehicles overseas as the global economy cools down. Its probably doubtful that U.S. auto makers will even hire more employees than they did in 2011 because the more cars they will sell the more "robots" they will put on the assembly line, the days of the auto makers being one of the larger employers in the country is over.

The auto makers are plagued with "corporate" malfeasance and the fact that it's easier to advertise than it is to do research and development and build a quality car. The U.S. auto industry is still suffering from the ills of the past and the problems that have haunted this industry just doesn't seem to want to go away any time soon and it's only a matter of time before more bankruptcies can be expected.

The days when the U.S. auto industry played a big role in the U.S. economy and provided millions of great paying jobs is over and once again "corporate America" has ruined an American icon. The U.S. auto industry will play a role in the economy in 2012 but will do little when it comes to creating jobs or rejuvenating the economy.

Technology and the tech world has certainly been a mixed bag for the "main street economy" as it seems that the world turns based on all these new electronic gadgets and American companies seem to be on top of their game when it comes to creating these toys. Hi-tech companies are producing huge profits and are doing very well on "Wall Street" but not so much when it comes to "main street".

People on "main street" feel as if they have to have these high priced gadgets in order to make their lives 'whole" even though many families are living close to the poverty line and can barely pay their bills. This means once again "corporate America" is taking billions out of the "main street economy" and reinvesting next to nothing. Once again this is "corporate facsism" doing its thing and "capitalism" taking a beating.

Hi-tech companies are creating these expensive toys in America but producing them in foreign countries depriving millions of Americans a job, this type of "corporate" behavior is just another reason why the "main street economy" will not recover anytime soon.

"Capitalism" doesn't work when "corporations" take huge amounts of money from "main street U.S.A." and reinvest that money on "Wall Street", Swiss bank accounts, the Kayman islands or in foreign countries. "Capitalism" only works when the money earned in a specific place is reinvested in that specific place. Hi-tech companies have taken trillions of dollars out of the "main street economy" and then distributed that money in foreign countries by manufacturing their products overseas instead of the "United States of America". The U.S. economy can't grow when most of our money spent on main street is distributed globally and not reinvested in this country, until we stop this type of business behavior the "main street" economy will continue to get worse.

Politicians are looking to the manufacturing sector to create jobs going forward and this is just not going to happen anytime in the near future as innovation, technology and cheap overseas labor will hinder any growth in manufacturing.

The U.S. auto industry re-hired some workers in 2011 and did hire some new workers, however their wages are half of that, that they made in 1980. We no longer have just real people working on assembly lines now, we have robots, now taking the place of American workers, wonder what they get paid?

The real problems in creating manufacturing jobs stems from the fact that the tech industry is the fastest growing sector in the economy and technology is creating millions of jobs, however not in the United States. Problem number two for manufacturing jobs in America is most manufacturers are 50-100 years old and in a down economy, both globally and domestically, they are more likely to lay off workers than do any hiring.

When politicians say they can create manufacturing jobs in "America they are either moronic or lying, because the prospects are minimal. Politicians in 2012 should be focusing on the real problems on main street that they can do something about, like a terrible corporate run health care system that most Americans don't want to use and can't afford.

HEALTH CARE

During the great health care debate of 2010 between President Obama and Congress it became perfectly clear that the American people were left entirely out of the debate. Two thirds of the American people want a health care system that they find easy to use and affordable and is available to all Americans. This very simple request never seems to penetrate the halls of Congress or the oval office.

There is nothing in this present health care system that can be saved or tweaked, the entire health care system has to go. The current health care system has become unaffordable and too dangerous to change or improve. The changes made to the health care system in 2010 did not accomplish any of the intended goals and only serves to bastardize the system even more.

Elected officials in this country have seemingly made up their minds on health care and are unwilling to listen to the American people. It's these same politicians that won't listen to the American people on issues relating to the economy on jobs and it's these same politicians who need to be looking for a job in 2013.

There are numerous reasons for voters to remove every member of Congress in the November 2012 elections with health care topping the list. Over the past thirty years the U.S. health care system has wasted more than fifteen trillion dollars denying people health care in this country while fifteen U.S. congresses and five U.S. presidents have each found a way to make the system worse. The fact that this country would deny any American health care is incredulous and inhumane yet in 2011 Ron Paul, a doctor no less, and a candidate running for president of the United States commented on television during a presidential debate that a dying individual without insurance or a means to pay should be allowed to die. This kind of evil and sinister comment uttered by a politician in 2011 proves that the health care system in this country is not in our hands.

When President Obama took office in 2009 he had the best opportunity of any president to scrap this terrible health care system and replace it with a "single payer" system but he turned his back on the American people and became part of corporate American instead. President Obama had the political capital and the support of two thirds of the American people to "shit can" this horrible "corporate" run health care system and replace it but chose to become a "corporate" puppet instead. The American people have wanted a new health care system in this country for fifty years and for fifty years members of congress have protected the "greedy corporations" that run the health care system in the country. From 2002-2010 health care costs in America doubled while at the same time "people" on "main street" have been taking pay cuts or losing their jobs. The average health care premium for a family in this country is over fourteen thousand dollars or about twelve hundred dollars a month and most of those policy's come with a five hundred or thousand dollar deductible. People in this country that have insurance are going without health care because they can't afford to pay the deductible. The American people can no longer afford "Wall Street" health care premiums on a "main street" budget.

The rising cost of health care can be attributed to many sources, however the blame for rising cost must be placed at the feet of the many corporations who run the health care system in this country and their CEO's. Corporate CEO's must know what a customer or patient is able to pay for their goods or services and be able to provide those goods and services for an acceptable price. The CEO's in the health care industry obviously didn't consider the ability of the patient to pay over the past decade and went the way of "greed" instead of reality. The U.S. health care industry has gone the way of the airline or auto industry and not paid attention to the needs of the American people.

Health care corporations were entrusted by the American people to provide them with quality and affordable health care and they have failed to do so. These CEO's haven't considered the what would be good for the health and welfare of the American people for the past ten years, they saw a recessionary economy and took every dollar out of the economy that they could before it collapsed. CEO's don't run their corporations on "main street" they operate on "Wall Street" where the money is and many Americans could care less except when it's about their health care.

The health care industry is a very close knit operation with many entangled partnerships and business agreements. By 2012 a small number of large health care corporations will own nearly the entire health care system and will form the biggest "monopoly" on "main street". By 2015 one large insurance company could employ or own twenty percent of all the hospitals, medical clinics, long term health care centers, re-hab centers, medical equipment manufactures, pharmaceuticals, and health care providers in the United States of America. One large insurance company could totally provide for all the health care needs for seventy million Americans and do over a half trillion dollars a year in sales. This means that when a consumers buys an insurance policy from "company alpha", that consumers will be obligated to have all their medical needs or services be provided by "company alpha". By 2015 there will be few if any choices to be made by the patient when it comes to health care. The patient will have no choice when it comes to the medical clinic they go to, they will have no choice when it comes to the hospital they go to, they will have no choice as to the rehab center there sent to and they will have no choice as to the pharmacy where they buy their drugs, if it doesn't say "company alpha" then their insurance policy will be no good. The American people have been backed into a corner when it comes to health care, they just don't know it yet.

Health care corporations have used the power given to them by congress to create enough chaos and confusion in the industry to insure that congress could never intervene and competitors could never compete. This is what the mortgage market managed to do before collapsing by creating CDS'S and derivatives that congress or no one else in the country could understand.

President Obama had good intentions when it came to health care reform, however he had no real clue what the problems were, and no ideal how to fix them. The presidents desire to insure every American was noble but some what off base because the current system already insured everyone, despite Ron Paul's statement that any American that can't pay for his health care shouldn't get health care, every American who needs health care has always gotten it if they wanted it. America has always had universal health care and all Americans have had access to that care, it's just that it's been paid for in many different ways. President Obama wanted to dignify health care for fifty million people, not pay for it because it was already paid for.

The health care debate becomes distorted and confusing because the political party's want it that way, the Democrats and Republicans want to throw the political football around for political advantage and not to fix the problems. President Obama needed to tell the American people that everyone in America got health care if they needed it and that many poor people used the health care system more than people with insurance would. The president needed to clear up the "myths" about health care and level with the American people but he didn't do it.

President Obama needed to explain to the American people that all Americans could and have used the health care system when sick or injured regardless whether they had insurance or money to pay. The president needed to explain how this health care was actually paid for or written off and who had to write it off but he didn't.

President Obama should have explained was how five hundred billion dollars is spent each year in this country denying people health care coverage. The American people don't want an insurance policy, they want an insurance card that provides for their health care needs. The "people" don't want a sixteen page document written in fine print that includes or excludes coverage, they want a card that gives them the health care that their physician deems necessary. The "people" don't want an insurance agent, they don't need T.V. advertising, they don't need people coming to their homes explaining the differences between two hundred different policy's, all the "people" want is health care when they need it at an affordable price.

Insurance company's waste hundreds of billions of dollars a year in unnecessary paper work trying to determine what customer is eligible for coverage and what coverage they are eligible for. Health care coverage should be broken down into two types of coverages, cosmetic and necessary and no American should be denied necessary coverage. Every American should be given the health care they need and every American should pay for selective cosmetic surgery. Health care coverage should not be akin to selecting options for a new automobile, health care should be given when needed.

The insurance company's have spent hundred of billions of dollars convincing the "people" that every American needs his own special health care policy tailored just for him or her, this has been used as a marketing device to justify the "corporate" health care system. The "corporations" running the health care system need to get together and design a one size fits all health care program. The goal of any health care system should be, good quality health care for all.

There should only be one insurance policy written in this country and that policy should cover every person in this country and become the law of the land. The health insurance industry would save hundreds of billions of dollars a year in not only paper work and advertising costs but in legal and accounting costs as well. Insurance company could certainly lobby congress for a system that features "arbitration" instead of "litigation" and probably would have the full support of the American people. "Arbitration" could cut billions every year off the cost of health care and would be far more fair to the health care system and the American people than the "litigation" system now in place.

A simple one policy one price health care system would also eliminate a large number of accounting procedures present in today's health care system. Every accounting step eliminated in the health care system would save money and time and make the system more efficient.

"Corporate America" screwed up the health care system in this country in the 1970's when CEOs in the health care industry discovered that there was lots of money to be made on "Wall Street", far more money than could be made by taking care of patients. It was then that the health care industry was turned into "a cash cow" for insurance companies and every sector of the health care industry.

There is no reason why anyone or any corporation should profit off health care, the health care workers should be paid for what they do and that should be the end of it. If we are to have a health care for profit system then it should not have even been introduced on "Wall Street" where millions of individuals have made trillions of dollars off the corporate run health care system. Every company in the health care industry could have remained a private company and put health care before profits and could have still done well financially.

"Wall Street" is not about health care, "Wall Street" is about increasing sales margins and profit and should never have become a part of the health care system.

The health care system we have in 2012 doesn't resemble the health care system we had in 1970 before it became "a Wall Street darling". The system we have today is far more expensive, more dangerous and far more conviluted.

In the 1970's doctors owned their own practices, rehab centers, long term care centers, and hospitals were owned by non-profit, and entrepreneurs tried to provide quality health care at a fair price. Pharmaceuticals were still working hard to provide lifesaving drugs and vaccines and equipment manufacturers were hard at work creating products for the health care industry that made things better for the doctors and patients.

In 2012 "corporate America" is taking over every sector in the health care industry and putting it under one umbrella in order to increase sales, up margins and double profits. Doctors are closing their practices and going to work for these "corporations" who are buying and building hospitals, buying up equipment manufacturers and franchising medical clinics like hamburger joints.

Mergers between these "corporate" vultures and pharmaceuticals will happen soon and it won't be long before a handful of "Wall Street" CEOs will own and operate the United States health care system.

The health care system in America is going the way of the financial system and in the near future could go the way of the financial system and crash just like the financial system did in 2008. There are many people in this country that feels the government shouldn't run anything, there are also many of us that believe "corporate America" can't run anything and we want "corporate America" out of the health care system sooner than later.

No American should want or need for his health care do be dictated in a board room full of CEOs trained in the banking business and if politicians don't get it, maybe they should listen to voices of the American people instead of reading their political playbook. Health care is still an issue in 2012 and will be until its put back into the hands of the entrepreneurs on "main street U.S.A. where it belongs.

THE NIXON DOCTRINE

In 1967 Richard Millhouse Nixon, a recent two time loser in American politics, wrote a manual of extreme importance known as the Nixon doctrine or by its more familiar name, the Republican playbook.

Dick Nixon was a masterful politician and had become very aware of the political vibes that embraced the nation. Dick Nixon after losing a bid to become Governor of California made a very enlightening statement declaring that the people would no longer have Dick Nixon to kick around anymore meaning he was through with politics.

When the political vibes in the nation changed, so did Dick Nixon's mind change, and he decided to run for president one more time. Anyone running for president needs a well drawn out plan or a political playbook and being a two time loser, not just any playbook. Dick Nixon designed his playbook around issues he knew he could win on, whether he believed in these issues or not.

Nixon knew that he would have more support in southern states than he would have in the north, so he came up with plan that would divide the country in half. Nixon understood that southerners would be blaming the democrats for passing the civil rights act in 1964 and that this could become an issue he could use to solidify his support in the south.

Dick Nixon was also talking with Jesse Helms and Strom Thurmund about shoring up support from born again Christians and how to frame that issue in the 1968 campaign. Dick Nixon was not into theology, however he knew some people who were theologians, and with their help created a message that would be palatable to evangelist.

Organized labor had played a huge role in his loss to John Kennedy in 1960 and Dick Nixon was not a forgiving man and he hated organized labor and was determined to even the score. Nixon knew that organized labor would campaign heavily and spend millions of dollars supporting Democrats and Hubert Humphrey, so he had to figure out a way to counter that attack. Nixon knew that "corporate America" and big business would not support a political party supported by organized labor, so Dick Nixon would openly court corporations for their support.

The National Rifle Association would be on board when Mr. Nixon would make his run for president and he expected them to help him win at least Montana and Wyoming for sure making him a viable candidate in at least five more northern states. The N.R.A. has always played a huge role in republican politics especially in tight elections where last minute money could make a difference.

The Republican party would always be supported by defense contractors because they hated the fact that organized labor had made inroads into their domain and democratic lawmakers were insisting that government contracts go to union shops—Nixon would know that he would have the upper hand on any issue concerning national defense because its defense contractors that dictate policy in the defense department. This explains why democrats are considered to be soft on national defense issues and why we went to war in Iraq and Afghanistan. Defense contractors only earn big dollars when America is at war and since Nixon defense contractors have always supported the Republican party.

When running for president in 1968 Dick Nixon would never have to worry about running out of money because anytime a Republican running for president needs money they just call on the corporate run health care industry. The corporate run health care system in America has given hundreds of billions of dollars to Republican candidates over the past century in order to insure that America never goes to a single pay, non-profit health care system. Health care debate in America is never about health care, but about saving a corporate run health care system that should never have existed in the first place, Republicans love it, the rest of the country hates it!!

The Nixon doctrine would not have been complete unless it called for de-regulation, the coal and oil industries have given billions of dollars over the years to any politician in Washington D.C. that would fight against regulatory controls. In order to satisfy their donors the Republican party has been the party of de-regulation for over a century.

Dick Nixon would run for president in 1968 and win using his newly formulated doctrine that would become the Republican playbook when Ronald Reagan added supply side economics to the doctrine in 1982.

The Nixon doctrine has been the source for the issues that Republican candidates have based their campaigns on since 1968, and for over 40 years in this country no politician has changed the debate. The Republican party uses the Republican playbook which exploits patriotism, religion, de-regulation, gun control, jobs, the civil rights act, organized labor, tax cuts and health care and since the Democrats don't have a playbook they simply run against the Republican playbook and the NEO cons.

For 45 years in this country the political issues have not changed and every two years those issues just become more polarized and the American people become more frustrated with politics. The sad truth about politics today is all you have to do to be a politician in America is to be a lawyer, have access to lots of money and read the Republican playbook and decide if you agree with it or you'll oppose it.

The politics of Dick Nixon and old Joe McCarthy have stood the test of time and have led to a divided nation ethnically and politically causing our government to become polarized and non-governing. Politically speaking this nation has become bias, bigoted, insensitive, vile, destructive, greedy and power mongering.

CANDIDATE OBAMA

Presidential candidate Barack Obama had such high hopes for America and the American people when running for president in 2008. Candidate Obama was to be the man who would unify the United States of America. The candidate Obama was going to undo the Nixon doctrine and the teachings of old Joe McCarthy which divided the country in half in 1968. Candidate Obama was touted by his supporters as a man who could bring this nation together and end the hatred feelings and the dissension that's existed between the north and the south since the civil rights act of 1964 or as some have felt since the election of 1860. Richard Nixon used these ill feelings that have stood the test of time to win an election for president in 1968 after writing the Nixon doctrine in early 1967.

Candidate Obama campaigned on the fact that he could bring people together and that he had the policy's and ideas that would play well in Washington D.C. and across the nation. Candidate Obama said he would reach across the aisle and make friends with the enemy and bring politics back into the 21st century. Candidate Obama was going to do what presidents Ford, Carter and Clinton couldn't do, unravel the Nixon doctrine. Candidate Obama promised the American people if elected that he would be different and would do the bidding of the American people and would not become a prisoner of the ideology of Washington D.C. and a political system owned and operated by "Wall Street".

Candidate Obama talked of bringing peace to a nation that's been at war for 25 out of the last 50 years or in case of a grade schooler, their whole life. the United States not only adopted the views of old Joe McCarthy but those views have become a major piece of our foreign policy. the neo-cons have had their way in this country for far too long and candidate Obama said he wasn't a neo con—

Candidate Obama seemed very concerned for the poor in this country and said that he had ideas on how to end poverty and strengthen the middle class, candidate Obama said that he had been a community organizer and understood the plight of the inner cities in America.

Candidate Obama campaigned saying he would overhaul the health care system and offer affordable health care for everyone on a universal basis. Candidate Obama promised universal health care that would treat every American in a fair and equal manner and with dignity and respect.

Candidate Obama promised an economic plan that would jump start an ailing economy and create jobs in America and build a stronger middle class. Candidate Obama lifted the hopes and aspirations of the poor in America that they might have more opportunity to build a better life for themselves and their families and share a slice of the American pie.

Candidate Obama promised the American people that he would rebuild the infrastructure in this great nation and insure that it would be safe for all Americans to use and enjoy.

Candidate Obama took an oath to defend and protect the United States of America against all that would do it harm and to serve it with honor.

Candidate Obama assured the American people that he was unlike other politicians, that he was different and that he would change things in Washington D.C., and that he would bring change to America.

Candidate Obama certainly knew what was wrong in America and said it very eloquently in some brilliant speeches said across America in a campaign that would win him the White House. In becoming president, candidate Obama has had to face the truth, the reality of running for president and the realizations of doing the job, have made for a very conflicting dream.

PRESIDENT OBAMA

No president has ever been able to predict what his presidency would be like or what he might accomplish as president, as the events of the day, determines the moves of tomorrow, and for any candidate running for president, to promise the American people anything is to deceive.

President Obama said he was a different kind of politician, however from the very beginning, that was not to be the case, President Obama followed the lead of all of his predecessors and rewarded his political cronies with jobs and top level positions in his administration. President Obama said he was going to change Washington D.C., instead he fortified it with the same old political faces that helped corrupt the place in the first place. As an American voting for President Obama you may have assumed that he would have cleaned house and made room for new people with new ideas and a yearning for change.

Politicians have their own definition of the word change and somewhere in their definition is the phrase "status quo". President Obama changed nothing in Washington D.C. when he named his cabinet, his advisors or his policies. President Obama merely switched from the old guard Republican administration to the old guard Democratic administration.

In 2008 the American people voted for change meaning that they wanted to see all new people in the executive branch of government and an all new way of doing things in Washington D.C. The American people wanted a president who would listen to them, and come to them for support and advice on major political issues, not to fight with an arrogant, belligerent, sarcastic and unyielding politicians.

President Obama had a majority in congress, a majority in the senate and the support of the people and instead of using that support to do the will of the American people, he chose to engage in a battle of wits with a moronic congress.

President Obama attempted to defy the Nixon doctrine and try to unify the politicians in congress and to reach across the aisle and seek compromise, Bill Clinton tried the same thing and ended up talking about Monica Lewinsky for half his term. In 2012 President Obama won't be talking about change and compromise, but staying the course and getting his majority back in the house and senate.

President Obama knows now that he needs the people in this country if he's to get re-elected and is now trying to re-connect with the American people, the ones he was elected to represent. The president if re-elected may listen to some of his old campaign speeches in which he talked of change and perhaps change the faces in Washington D.C. instead of re-cycling them.

President Obama promised to end the wars in Iraq and Afghanistan if elected and he has fulfilled a half of that promise, but what about fulfilling the whole promise. The president doesn't need the approval of congress to end a war, so why are we still in Afghanistan?, accomplishing nada.

Candidate Obama vowed to help the poor and middle class improve their lives and to give those living in poverty a second chance. President Obama has seen more people slip into poverty and watched as the middle class has moved ever so close to the poverty line.

Businesses have a business model to go by and this helps the owner determine the status of his business, when an owner notices that his business model is not working, he either has to change the way he's doing business or go bankrupt, the American family has a financial model that they must deal with and most families have had to change their financial model several times and for many families they have tweaked their financial model for the final time and the next step is bankruptcy.

Mr. President the financial model for the average American family doesn't work any longer, 30 years of stagnant wages and rising cost have put most middle class Americans at a point of no return and out of options, in 2012 44 million middle class Americans could fall into poverty and at least that many more in 2013.

President Obama if re-elected must know that for the average middle class American family to be able to stay in the middle class wages have to go up or expenses have to come down or both need to happen.

President Obama vowed to help the middle class and the poor, however the middle class is shrinking and the poverty level is rising, that's not helping the middle class and the poor. The president never mentions "corporate America" when he talks about job losses in the United States or the fact that "corporate America" has stolen from the "middle class" and the poor and given to the rich and "Wall Street". The president doesn't seem to know why the economy is in the toilet and that its his new corporate friends and donors that's put the economy in the toilet. Mr. President, if elected, you need to get some new friends and have security toss all your old corporate buddies out of the country, you know the place where they prefer to do business!!!

THE 21ST CENTURY

Though 11 years removed, politicians in 2012 seem to be firmly entrenched in the politics of the 20th century and "the Nixon Doctrine". At a time when "main street U.S.A." is mired in a depression politicians are talking about neo-con politics and social issues, which will have no bearing on whether 1/2 of the American people could be living in poverty by 2013.

While 300 million Americans are questioning what their lives will be like in 2016, politicians running for office are questioning what their political parties will look like in 2016.

While "main street" Americans are worried about their ability to support their families, politicians are concerned about, how best to portray their opponents as unworthy of being Americans. Divisive politics will not solve the problems that are engulfing those American families trying to keep their heads above water in a depressing economy. "Main street" Americans need worry, when politicians in 2012 fight over the Nixon doctrine which was written in 1967 instead of discussing ideas which might get the American people out of the financial quandary they find themselves in, in 2012.

America needs its president and members of congress to understand the needs of its people in the 21st century and to share a positive vision for the country going forward. The vision must be about "main street" and the people of this country, not big business, corporations and "Wall Street", these have been the villains that have done the damage to "main street U.S.A."

President Obama has a passion for meeting with the business leaders in the country in order to find solutions on how increase business and create jobs on "main street", the president doesn't get it, these are the individuals that have run these 50-100 year old businesses and created the depression on "main street". These business leaders ran out of new ideas decades ago, if they have any ideas on fixing the "main street" economy, why haven't they done it already. Most CEO's and company presidents have never run a business on "main street" or even had a real job, these individuals are mostly silverspoons who are life deprived and mentally deficient.

The status quo will no longer work for "the main street economy" President Obama and members of congress need to act fast and be progressive by implementing programs needed to stimulate "the main street economy" and keep it going.

"The main street economy" and all its entities must be rebuilt from the ground up and that means by starting with those living in poverty and those about to fall into poverty. 50 million people living in poverty in the United States of America is certainly a black eye on the greatest nation on earth and the prospects of 88 million people living near the poverty line is even more scandalous. What these figures illustrate is, even if every American who needs a job gets one, the level of poverty in this country will not improve significantly.

The president and members of congress aren't talking about poverty, there talking about jobs and the unemployment numbers, jobs are important however creating 10 million jobs will do no good unless those jobs pay "a living wage". $10.00 an hour jobs will not ease the poverty problem in America, earning $10.00 an hour and trying to support a family means you will stay in poverty, not have an opportunity to get out of poverty. Two bread winners in a family both working full time and paying a baby sitter would have to each make over $15.00 an hour to stay above the poverty line in most states.

The leaders of this country don't get it, their CEO friends and business leaders in this country are not going to pay their employees "a living wage" unless they are forced to and then they won't pay anymore than necessary. 1/2 of the American people are living pay check to pay check or at the poverty line and "corporate America" doesn't give a damn because "corporate America" has no idea of what they have done to "main street U.S.A." when for 40 years they have devalued the pay check of the American worker. If all "corporate America" has to offer the American people are jobs that pay "a now living wage" then the American worker does not need "corporate America" doing business on the streets of America.

RIGHT TO WORK LAWS

Wisconsin is pretty much a typical American state and mostly middle class, however the median income in Wisconsin is only $28,500 while the danger line for a middle class family of four falling into poverty is $41,000.00 Governor Scott Walker of Wisconsin wants to lower taxes and reduce the income of government workers, what Governor Walker is doing is creating a scenario by which the great state of Wisconsin becomes an impoverished state with many of its residents living in poverty. No state can increase revenues to pay bills by cutting taxes and slicing wages, the math doesn't work, there's governors in this country running their states with a political playbook instead of using sound economic principals.

Governor Walker is running his state using the political principals being touted by two billionaire oil barons, the Koch brothers, whose desire it is, to eliminate regulatory controls, and destroy the middle class. The Koch brothers have no respect whatsoever for the environment and feel that the only purpose for the poor and middle class in this country is to serve the rich.

The Koch brothers support Governor Walker in Wisconsin and any governor or politician who will support "right to work laws" or de-regulation, the Koch brothers have no respect for the American workers who worked for them or for the American consumer who bought their product and made them billionaires.

The wealthy have a tendency to forget where they came from and what it took to make them rich, and with a short term memory, it's easy for them to turn on the people who made them successful. There would be few millionaires and billionaires in this country had no consumer bought their products or no one would work for them!!, without employees or consumers few businesses in America could stay open and make a profit.

Back in the 1960's and 70's business owners would not only want to pay their employees "a living wage" but they would also share some of their profits by giving those any employees raises and more benefits, now all you have are CEO's and wealthy businessmen, paying their employees "a now living wage" and sharing their profits with stockholders and politicians.

Governor Walker of Wisconsin and other governors supported by the Koch brothers who support "right to work laws" in their states have zero respect for the workers of their state and are putting their states in a position down the line to become impoverished.

> "Right to work laws mean you have the right to work for nothing and the right to be fired for no reason!!

Governors know that "right to work laws" create poverty and the more low paying jobs a state has the more poverty will be created, so what's the motive for encouraging low income jobs, it's to satisfy "corporate America and their donors. These governors owe their jobs to big business in this country and they don't give a damn about the working class in their state or what their state will look like in 20 years.

Governor McDonnell of Virginia went on T.V. boasting of convincing a business from Maryland to move to Virginia and saying he created X amount of jobs, the governor in affect was ruining those good paying jobs in Maryland and creating nothing jobs in Virginia. Governor McDonnell has a real problem when it comes to business, he doesn't understand how it works, and neither does any governor supporting right to work laws.

Jobs that don't pay "a living wage" are not needed in the United States in 2012, there are 40 million of these jobs in the country today and it's because of those jobs that 30 million people are living in poverty today.

In the 1960's and 70's ten percent of the jobs in America paid "a non living wage" in 2012 fifty percent of the jobs in America pay "a non living wage", that's because "corporate America" has destroyed the good paying jobs in the country and replaced them with low paying jobs.

"Corporate America" can not be forced to pay the American worker "a living wage" however, the members of congress can pass legislation increasing the "minimum wage" to $12.00 an hour and not only allow some of the people living in poverty to have a little better life, but that would also put billions of dollars back into "the main street economy", without any government spending. Increasing the "minimum wage" to $12.00 an hour would "jump start" "the main street economy" by invigorating the economy and creating jobs. "Demand" for goods and services can not be created until the people have some "extra" cash to spend and by increasing the "minimum wage" 40 million Americans will have lots more money to spend.

"Corporate America" and "Wall Street" has prospered while the American people have learned how to live on less and at no time in the last 40 years has big business thrown a bone to the working man in this country and now there are governors who still want to take even more from the people there suppose to represent.

The rationale for lowering wages in this country when the median incomes in most states are below the poverty line is pure delusional and if the main street economy is to be fixed and jobs are to be created the first and most important step would be to increase "the minimum wage".

THE MINIMUM WAGE

"The federal minimum wage" was passed by members of congress to insure that sweat shops would never exist in the United States of America and to protect against indigence. Politicians have taken the "minimum wage" legislation one step farther, they have used the minimum wage as a tool to advance a political agenda and satisfy their donors. The "minimum wage" was never intended to become "a wage", it was supposed to be a starting point or an entry level wage, paid to an employee for a brief period of time.

"Corporate America" with the support of their political friends redefined the meaning of the "minimum wage" legislation and have used it to create massive profits by taking full advantage of the American work force. In the 1960's and 70's it was "corporate America" that used the "minimum wage" to force the self employed in this country out of business because they were paying their employees "a living wage" and couldn't compete with the corporate discounters.

In 2012 50 million people are living in poverty and many of those are living in poverty because of the minimum wage that was supposed to prevent poverty in this country. The fact is "the minimum wage law" couldn't prevent those individuals form falling in to poverty because the current minimum wage is not "a living wage". The poverty line in the country is said to be $23,000.00 a year and a person working full time making minimum wage will only earn $15,000.00 a year.

"Minimum Wage"

1. The lowest wage, determined by law or contract that an employer may pay an employee for a specified job.

2. "A living wage"

The American Heritage Dictionary

"A living wage" by any standard would have to be a wage earned that couldn't be considered indigence or unworthy.

Washington D.C. politicians have been disrespectful of the poor for decades, saying they won't work or they prefer to be on the dole, the truth is millions of Americans living in poverty do work full time. Our founding fathers would have never wanted to see an American worker with a full time job living in poverty, however that doesn't seem to bother today's leaders in congress.

President Obama and members of congress running for re-election are all talking about creating jobs, and fixing "the main street economy" but not one has mentioned increasing the "minimum wage" and giving 40 million needy workers a raise. "The main street economy" needs a major stimulus and there's nothing better to jump start "the main street economy" than an increase in the "minimum wage".

Politicians need know that even if 10 million jobs were created on "main street" and the unemployment numbers fell back to 4% that the poverty numbers would stay the same and the number of Americans living paycheck to paycheck wouldn't change. The American worker needs his paycheck to increase in order to keep up with the cost of living while "corporate America" is making every attempt to deflate wages.

"Corporate America" continues its assault on the American worker and the economy on "main street" continues to get worse while members of congress and the president continues to protect their corporate friends and CEO's.

The American people continue to suffer while politicians protect "corporate America" blinded to the fact that "corporate America" is not the solution to the economic difficulties on "main street" they are the problem.

"Corporate America" will not increase wages on "main street" even though gas and food prices are going higher and the cost of health care has doubled in 10 years. "Corporate America" does not care that 50 million people are living in poverty because they won't pay their employees "a living wage" and "corporate America" doesn't care about the American people living paycheck to paycheck because their deflating wages on "main street".

Americans need jobs that are worth having and if members of congress were representing the American workers in this country instead of big business there would be jobs worth having in the country and every job would pay "a living wage" and no child would go to bed hungry at night.

The president and members of congress could play a role in jump starting "the main street economy" and giving millions of Americans an opportunity to rise above the poverty line by simply increasing the minimum wage to $12.00 an hour.

MAIN STREET U.S.A.

Main Street U.S.A., home to 300 million people and a declining economy, "main street U.S.A., where ½ of the people are living in or close to the poverty line. Main street U.S.A. where people go to work if they have a job and work for what "corporate America" thinks they are worth.

"Corporate America" home to millionaires and billionaires who run the businesses on "main street" and then send the money to "Wall Street". "Corporate America" the ones who decide what life will be like for the 300 million Americans living on "main street U.S.A."

The people who do the work on "main street U.S.A." gets paid what ever "corporate America" wants to pay them and it's those wages that determines the economic conditions on "main street U.S.A.", and how the people on "main street U.S.A." lives.

In 2012 138 million people on "main street U.S.A." are living near the poverty line or living in poverty, meaning that "corporate America has depressed the wages of the workers in this country, until half the American people are nearly living in "the poor house.

THE REASON

"Corporate America" has deflated wages on "main street U.S.A. so severely that there are fewer jobs on main street that pay "a living wage".

Federal, state and local taxes are very much affected by wages paid on "main street U.S.A." when wages are kept artificially low then the tax revenue goes down and the deficit goes up. "Corporate America" causes a huge hardship on social programs by not paying "a living wage" to its employees forcing the government to supplement wages, this in essence means the federal, state and local governments are subsidizing "corporate America" and making up the difference in wages between what "corporate America" pays an employee and what it cost low wage earners to live.

"A minimum wage" increase would lessen the burden on social programs and increase government revenues and make it possible for low wage earners to buy food and clothing, a winning scenario for everyone, even for the corporations who would pay these additional wages.

By "corporate America" depressing wages for 30 years "main street U.S.A." has been put in a very bad way, as well as the U.S. tax structure, Americans would not need as much government assistance and tax revenues would be much higher if wages were not depressed.

Making "main street U.S.A." whole again can only be accomplished in two ways, either wages go up or prices come down, and the latter will not happen.

In 2012 with 138 million Americans living in or near the poverty line it's clear that creating 10-15 million jobs won't fix the problem, that might help 30% of the people flirting with the poverty line but do nothing for the other 100 million people. Jobs alone will not fix the economy on "main street" and when it's more than likely that "corporate America" will create less jobs in 2012 going forward than more jobs, "main street" Americans have very little to look forward to if politicians can't force "corporate America" to increase wages.

"Corporate America has an oil industry that refuses to take the necessary steps to lower oil and gas prices and make the United States dependent from foreign oil.

Every honest oil man or corporate CEO, explains in detail what the energy policy should be in the United States but no politician wants to do what they are saying to do. Politicians are bought and paid for by the dishonest oil companies and the Koch brothers who tell members of congress what to do and when to do it.

A number of oil company executives current and former have an energy plan that would not only lower oil and gas prices but would get us out of OPEC as well.

AN ENERGY PLAN

America gets about 3 million barrels of oil from Canada every day, if politicians were nicer to Canada, Canada could supply the United States with $4^{1/2}$ million barrels a day.

If the American people would respect the people and government of Mexico, the United States could get 1-2 million barrels of oil a day from Mexico.

Oil producers in America are only producing 7 million barrels of oil a day and they can produce 10 million barrels of oil a day if they wanted to or were made to in order to get more oil leases.

By using natural gas resources and corn, refiners could save up to 2 million barrels of oil a day by creating methanol or ethanol to be used in flex fuel vehicles.

By requiring all commercial and government vehicles to be run on natural gas by 2016, would save at least 3 million barrels of oil a day.

By requiring auto makers to make autos that get 40 miles a gallon by 2016 would save another 2 million barrels of oil a day.

This simple energy plan would mean that by 2016 the United States of American would be producing 3 million barrels of oil more than it needs and make the country dependent from foreign oil.

ISSUES

"Main street U.S.A." the forgotten culture in American politics, they seem to show up every two years to patronize us and give us hope, but then they get elected and go away for two years, politicians that is. "Main street U.S.A." has issues and if the gypsy's from Washington D.C. believe that the elections of 2012 will be business as usual, they may be dead wrong.

November 6 2012, the people will have the opportunity to go to the polls and get rid of every member of congress and then they will have the opportunity to become a soldier in "the war of 2012" and insure that every new member of congress understands that they were elected to do what's right for the people on "main street, not the people on "Wall Street".

"We the people" of this country have issues and "we the people" want those issues addressed in a positive and speedy manner.

We have an issue with politicians who treat the less fortunate people in this country with total disrespect and ire. Every American has the right to be treated with dignity and respect and to have their needs attended to in a humane manor by every elected representative or government. Politicians should note; they represent all the people not just their political base and those who don't represent all the people, need to be re-called.

The people on "main street" do not appreciate some holier than thou politician lecturing them about money, morals or religion and the people of this country should not be blamed in any way for the economic "mess" created on "main street" by "corporate America."

The people on "main street" will take issue with any politician who chooses to use our young as "cannon fodder" for any new pre-emptive war like Vietnam, Afghanistan or Iraq. The president and members of congress shall never again listen to or accept money from any defense contractor or oil company executive when making a decision on whether the United States of America ever goes to war again.

The people on "main street" have presented an energy policy to the congress that will exempt us from buying oil from our enemies and OPEC forever. The peoples energy policy is endorsed by former and current oil executives who believe the policy will bring down prices and make the country dependent from all foreign oil.

The people on "main street" want a health care "option" so that we might opt out of the grossly expensive and dangerous "corporate run health care system we have now. The current "corporate run health care system" is so convoluted and corrupted with fraud that if not fixed, it will collapse, and create the same kind of financial crisis that "the Mortgage crisis" of 2008 did.

The people want "a high speed rail system" in this country like all the rest of the modern nations in the world has. We don't want to have to drive 3 hours to catch an airplane and have to wait 2 hours to take off, then have to wait 2 more hours during a lay over. We no longer want to have to sit in a seat made for the "thin man" and have to listen to babies cry for 5 hours. We no longer want to have to check the weather report or question if our plane will be ready to take off on time or not. We the people no longer want to deal with CEO's and corporations who form monopolies and dictate how we travel, we want a high speed rail system.

"A high speed rail system" would create millions of good paying jobs across the country and would energize a 150 year old transportation system that's old and out of gas.

The people on "main street" wants co-ops that could provide us with American made goods and an option to a 60 year old food industry that keeps raising prices and filling their food with grain and air. Nationally run co-ops would compete with "corporate America" and provide "a living wage" for its employees while putting the "made in the U.S.A." tags and labels back on our furniture and in our clothing.

We the people have issues with paying gas taxes and having those taxes used for other things, we don't have a problem with the tax, we have a problem with that tax money not being used for infrastructure projects. President Eisenhower gave us the federal highway system in 1957 with the feeling that future president's would take care of it, what happened?

When states collect gasoline taxes those taxes should go immediately to repair their roads and bridges and if those taxes aren't enough to make their bridges and road safe, then increase the tax. The president should order all federal highways and bridges to be inspected and those with serious safety concerns should be fixed, no questions asked. The debate in congress should never be about spending on infrastructure, it should be about how soon.

Infrastructure spending and rules were written into the 1957 highway act, whether in words or spirit and it's time elected officials did their job. The rebuilding of our roads and bridges would create millions of good paying jobs in every part of the country and keep our citizens safe.

Government officials should note that giving contracts to large construction firms will probably not create any new jobs for "American workers" as these companies will go with the help they have or hire immigrant workers, this has been the case forever and won't change. Large construction companies and their lawyers know how to skirt provisions in a contract that says the corporations must only hire American workers or must pay a certain "minimum wage" as agreed to. "Corporate america" is about profit and not jobs or wages and they know how to turn a government contract into a "cash cow".

We the people see no issue with "the main street economy" creating 60 million new good paying jobs in the next two years or by the congressional elections in 2014.

The president and members of congress need only, increase the minimum wage to "a living wage, increase infrastructure spending, get rid of corporate run health care, create co-ops, build a high speed rail system nationwide, forbid states to pass right to work laws and mandate that all commercial and government vehicles run on natural gas by 2016.

Do these things and "the main street economy" will grow again, 138 million Americans will see the light of day and the middle class will become strong again, sat around and do nothing. By 2016 there will be no middle class.

THE AMERICAN WORKER

In 2012 the American worker is paying the full price for political intervention into the work place on "main street U.S.A." In the beginning or back in the 1940's and 50's. The Democrats took the side of organized labor while the Republican party stood up for big business, at the time the stock market was merely a casino for the rich. During the 1940's, 50's and 60's the Democrats would get major support from organized labor and with the political support from the Democrats organized labor grew stronger and stronger. In those 3 decades big business could not match the money or influence generated by organized labor and the union movement grew rapidly, this would begin to change in the 1970's when the new generation of corporations began to take-over the business landscape on "main street" and "Wall Street" would begin to flourish and become relative in the U.S. economy.

In 1981 Ronald Reagan the newly elected president from California would join with big business and "Wall Street" and begin to turn around the momentum that organized labor had created and this was the beginning of the downfall of the American worker. President Reagan, big business and "corporate America" would take away the mojo enjoyed by organized labor and would begin to stymie the wages and benefits of the American worker. As "corporate America" took over all the businesses on "main street" the wages and benefits of the American workers would stagnate for 30 years.

"Corporate America" and the Republican party would now do to the American worker and their families for 30 years what the Democrats and organized labor and done to big business for 30 years, make their lives miserable.

In 2012 both political parties have had their own way for 30 years each, now is the time to de-politicize the American work force and re-energize the American work force. Politics and the economy will never mesh well and is the reason for the ups and downs in the U.S. economy and after 60 years of interference by the political system it's time to quit playing political games with the economy and let the economists do their thing. The Republican party and "Wall Street" have won the war, the American worker is on his hands and knees begging for mercy and food, so the white flag has been presented and a truce has been called for, so let's begin, both Democrats and Republicans to re-build "the main street economy" that "Wall Street" and "corporate America" has destroyed.

CLASS WARFARE

In 2012 the wealthy in this country are claiming to be the victims of "class warfare" and the 99% of the have nots in this country are treating them un-fairly. The message being sent in 2012 by the 99% to the 1% is clear, we the American people have been abused and taken advantage of long enough, and yes we will engage in "class warfare" against the 1% and we will fight to the end.

The 1% in this country may have the wealth and the power in this country, however the American people have the numbers, so it should be an even fight. The 1% started this fight in 1970 when they began to take the wealth off "main street" and put it on "Wall Street" and the American people have not forgotten, while the 1% whine and say they are victims, we the 99% will be fighting to get our money back.

"Class warfare" in the 21st century will be about more than just money, it's going to be about dignity and respect and about the rights that have been taken away from us by the 1%. We want our politicians free from corporate influence and from the power of the wealthy. We want our elected officials to once again represent all the American people and not just the chosen few who have the most to give in political campaigns. We want the president and members of congress to spend their time making our communities better, when more attention is paid to "main street" and less to "Wall Street" then we'll know, they are beginning to get the message.

"Class warfare" in the 21st century is about lifting 50 million Americans out of poverty and giving another 100 million Americans the ability to avoid poverty and save the "middle class" in this country from becoming extinct. We will not allow the 1% to destroy "the main street economy" completely and render the "middle class" irrelative.

We plan to restore "capitalism" in the country in the 21st century which was taken away by "corporate America" and return the economic system on "main street" to a "capitalist" system, under "capitalism" the 1% could have never ruined "the main street economy" and become the 1%. In a "capitalist" form of government wealth is distributed and profits are re-invested and the economy keeps growing and the wealth remains where it was created.

"Class warfare" is about our founding fathers meaning of the words "all men are created equal" and the 1%'s translation of those words to mean that with wealth comes power and with power comes certain "unalienable" rights not given to those with lesser means.

"Class warfare" has been part of the American culture for a long time and it's not going away when the 1%'s call for a truce.

In the 1960's there was "class warfare" when a majority of whites in the south re-belled against the civil rights acts which gave equal rights to all Americans.

In the 1960's during the Vietnam war and a time when America had a draft and every young American was expected to do his duty to his country it was very apparent that there was a large number of "silverspoons" sitting on the sidelines, ignoring their civic duties.

"Class warfare" was happening in the 1970's when it took and an act of congress to guarantee every woman in America the right to a surgical abortion. The wealthy females in the country had always enjoyed this privilege, they could find a willing doctor or could suddenly fly out of country and have the abortion, while the poor in the country used a coat hanger.

"Class warfare" in the 80's was about a group of holier than thou's who went on "a morality binge" declaring that if you weren't one of them, then you must be one of _____?? We are "one people", "one country", this country should not be a class divided between believers and non believers.

"The class warfare" between workers and employers has created a huge "disparity of wealth" in the country, as the wealthy has used the middle class and the poor in the country as laborers and servants and consumers for the past 30 years and have not shared that wealth with the people they have taken it from. The old phrase "working class" has rooted itself in American culture and become a major player in "the class warfare" feud.

In the 90's "class warfare" would be about the distribution of wealth from the rich to the poor, or from the haves and the have nots. Once again the rich in this country has a habit of forgetting how they got rich, they got rich because they were able to hire the have nots in this country to produce or manufacture their goods or services and they got rich because the have nots in the country purchased their goods and services. The American people were there for them and their families when they were acquiring their wealth but when they are asked to give something back to the less fortunate they cry like infants and act like "greedy bastards".

In the 21st century the "greedy bastards" are once again whining about "class warfare" when the "occupy" movement calls them "one percenters" and they say it's "class warfare" and divisive.

Yeah! It's "class warfare" and what about it, the "greedy bastards" have been waging "class warfare" against the 99% of Americans forever and it's about time the 99% stood up and went to war against the one percent that controls all the money and power in this country.

"Class warfare" evolves on a number of fronts in this country, not just the 99% versus the 1%, but with social and moral issues as well. Americans have chosen sides and become deeply divided into a number of "classes", the high class, the middle class, the working class and the different religious classes, "class warfare" is part of the American culture, much to the chagrin of our founding fathers who believed that "all men are created equal" and should be treated with dignity and respect, even if all Americans can't agree with our founding fathers elected officials should agree and uphold their wishes, as they are sworn to do.

THE WAR

50 years ago we had a Catholic president named John Fitzgerald Kennedy, everyone was in love with and enchanted by "Camelot". The world was at peace and the country was growing rapidly with new communities popping up everywhere and older communities were being revitalized.

Elvis Presley was the king, the corvette was "the sports car" and the New York Yankees were nearly unbeatable and the economy was booming. Those days seemed so simple yet so robust and there was no doubt that these were the "good times.

50 years later we are discussing the prospects of a Mormon president, their is no Camelot we have been at war for over 10 years, the countries growth has slowed greatly, many of our communities are old and filled with blight, the king is dead, sports cars are just for the one percenters, the Yankees can't even buy a World Series and the economy is trashed, so much for the good times.

America is not the country it was 50 years ago economically, socially or politically, quite frankly, America in 2012 is not what it used to be and that's sad, especially for the younger generation. In 2012 we know where we are as our economy on "main street" stinks, our political system sucks and our morals have flown out the window.

America is overdue for a peaceful revolution, not like Libya or Syria, God only knows we don't need anymore wars in which our young are maimed or killed. We need a war that changes the way we do business on "main street" and we need a war that makes "main street U.S.A.", "whole again". We need a war that takes back the power and the influence from the one percenters and gives it back to the 99% of Americans that don't live on "Wall Street" or in Washington D.C.

Politicians and "corporate America" has had its way with the American people way to long and now it's time for the American people to have their way with politicians and "corporate America".

"Corporate America" has ruined the economy on main street U.S.A. while members of congress have given their full support to any CEO whose wanted it. Our challenge as Americans will be to undo "corporate America" with boycotts and protests and to defeat every member of congress in November 2012.

We ask our fellow Americans to join us now or in the future in an effort to take back the power given to us by our founding fathers that's been taken from us by politicians, the Supreme Court and "corporate America".

We the people who live on "main street U.S.A." must know that "the main street economy" will not recover this year or never unless we the people do something about it.

We have told the members of congress and the president what they could do to jump start "the main street economy" and create 60 million good paying jobs. However we know they are going to support the 1% percenters and not give a damn about us, because they have to do what the 1% percenters tell them to do.

We the people can if unified get rid of every politician and lobbyist in Washington D.C. in November 2012 and do what the people of Canada did in 1993 to their parliament, the people of Canada ousted the conservative Tory party, and allowed the liberals to govern alone for 2 years. The Tory party didn't whine about it, they did what's right and listened to the Canadian people and the people put them back into power after they changed their party platform to conform with what the people wanted.

We the people can change our government the same way the people in Canada did by voting out an entire political party or by voting against every incumbent in this years election. We can join as one and unify or we can accept the status quo and be held hostage by "corporate America" and their political advocates. The American people can change their government every two years if they wish, the Canadian people are glad they did in 1993, the American people might be very pleased if they do it on November 6, 2012.

For 50 years 10's of millions of entrepreneurs and small businessmen have sought to make a living or create a dream for ourselves. For 50 years we have run our businesses and have observed the other businesses among us. We have talked to the owners and managers of thousands of businesses and to many district managers of competing corporate stores. We watched everyday as more and more corporate stores would open on "main street" and more and more of us went out of business. For us who survived we have watched as "the main street economy" went from "bustling" to "bust".

We have been both privileged and honored to have been part of "the main street economy" for all these years and we feel very fortunate to have been able to hire 10's of thousands of employees over those years and been able to pay them "a living wage" and provide them with a good work place.

We are proud of what we were able to do for the American workers and it saddens us greatly to see what's become of the business landscape on "main street" in 2012. For many years business would get better and better; especially between the years of 1950 to 1980, then in 1980 things began to slow down with smaller increases in revenue and higher product cost. From 1980 to 2000 business seemed to stay about the same with corporate stores opening everyday and more privately owned businesses closing.

For us who owned our first businesses in the 1950's we had seen the handwriting on the wall for a long time, we knew what the "corporate revolution" would do to "main street" and we knew our days in business were numbered. We also fully understood what a corporate take over of the businesses on main street would mean, we knew that some day "the main street economy" would collapse, and in 2005 "the main street economy" finally did collapse.

Economist and politicians won't agree that "the main street economy" collapsed in 2005 because they never worked on "main street" and they don't understand "the main street economy". Economist and politicians are only concerned about the GDP and the S&P, they don't give a damn about the economy where the regular people live.

In 2005 we called the switchboard in Washington D.C. and was able to talk to the individuals who work in the offices of the different congressmen and senators in congress and we wanted to tell them how bad the economy actually was.

We told the people we talked to that "the main street economy was in a deep recession and that it wouldn't be long before there would be a major financial crisis in the country similar to the one in California in the late 1980's, in which un-employment went to 16%, banks failed and housing prices dropped in half.

It was clear to us who still was running businesses in this country competing against "corporate America" that the economy on "main street" was in dire straights. Politicians and economist in 2012 still don't get it, they believe that when things get back to where they were in 2008, everything will be good again, guess again, in 2008 the main street economy was in the toilet.

"The main street economy" is and has been in a major recession since 2005 and if the American people don't rise up and fight, "the main street economy" will never come out of the recession it's in.

"Corporate America" is in total disarray, it's aging, "corporate America" as we know it is 50-150 years old, its lost its luster. In the 1960's and 70's "corporate America" had some new toys, like the fast food industry, the food was delivered fast and it was "cheap" and it had appeal; because it was new and different—50 years later the food is still delivered fast, however it's the same old food and in 2012, it's not cheap. Fast food is becoming more expensive because sales are decreasing and in order to keep their top line viable, prices are going up.

Corporate run clothing retailers face real challenges going forward as on line sales have continued to cut into store sales, meaning that the traditional department store may become nothing more than a "showroom". Clothing sold on line can have far less in the way of profit margins built in meaning profit margins for department store retailers will shrink over the years. Department store are way over-built in most areas meaning that more stores will close than open in the coming years causing many job losses in the future. The future for clothing retailers is not good and their participation in the economy on "main street" is dwindling.

The discounters and big box stores own much of the business on "main street" in 2012, however what they offer "the main street economy is far more negative than positive. They have driven down prices to a point that their competitors can't compete and they don't pay their employees "a living wages", so the jobs they provide for the American workers are meaningless.

Corporate run home improvement stores are no better for "the main street economy" than the big box stores and the discounters, they have run their competition out of business by selling foreign made "crap" and paying their help next to nothing.

The auto industry has aged much like the rest of "corporate America", in the 1960's and 70's the automobile was the "coolest" thing in America and the U.S. auto makers made real "classics", in 2012 they make real "generics". The American people are tired of buying high price pieces of junk that won't out run the monthly payments, no one wants to still have to make payments on a car that won't run. The U.S. auto makers still don't get it, we want a good quality car at a fair price, we don't want a car that looks good in a television commercial but won't last 100,000 miles.

The corporate run housing industry is dead in the water for the next 2-3 years because it cost more to build a house than they can sell one for and until building cost come down and prices go up the housing market will continue to stay in the doldrums.

The corporate run health care system gets more expensive everyday and is killing more people than it ever has. The current health care system is being run by people with out a clue, the cost for health care is outrageous and convilutive and more people are dying of infections they get in the hospital each day. The entire health care system is about to come apart and cause a huge financial and social disaster.

"Corporate America" has destroyed "the main street economy" and will soon destroy the U.S. Economy if the lawmakers in Washington D.C. don't act soon. {"Corporate America" is old and out of touch with reality and the CEO's running "corporate America" are not in it, to make these corporations better, they are in it for the money they can take out of it. "Corporate" CEO's have no skin in the game and no real ties or feelings for the corporations that they are running, it's all about the bottom line and the power.

Technology which could have been a real bright spot for "the main street economy" has turned into a negative because even though the innovation for their products are created in America the products are produced overseas meaning American workers get nothing while "Wall Street" gets all the profits.

"Main street" gets nothing while "Wall Street gets everything and now "corporate America" is falling apart "piece by piece", this is not the America that we dreamed about, however this is the America that we have.

Politicians and corporations have created the America we have today and if we the American people want a different America and a better America, it's time to stand up and fight!!!

THE WAR OF 2012

We the American people have the opportunity to make America the country we want it to be, we can unite, and become good soldiers and fight in the war to restore American to greatness in 2012.

We will make America great again by imploring politicians to once again represent the American people instead of "Wall Street". By demanding that corporations produce quality products made in the U.S.A. by American workers. By ridding the country of corporate run health care and guarantying that every American gets good quality and inexpensive health care. By ensuring that the United States of America never again engages in pre-emptive wars that kill and maim our young and ruin our economy. By getting rid of right to work laws that ask the American worker to work for "a non living wage" and have no job security. By demanding that the federal minimum wage be increased to "12.00 an hour. By demanding that lawmakers invest in our infrastructure and environment in order to make our streets and air better for our citizens. By having the government invest in high speed rail, co-ops and job training programs that will create the jobs of the future.

We Americans are proud of our country and we will fight for our country, even if it means over turning our political system and telling "corporate America" to go to hell.

"The war of 2012" begins with demands that will make America the country it used to be before the corporation revolution and take it back to the days when all Americans shared in the wealth not just the 1%.

We all own a small piece of America and we will fight to make that small piece worth what it was in the 1950's and 60's when "capitalism" and the American dream was achievable.

> "Corporate America" declared war on the American people forty years ago and the time has come for the "people" to fight back. "Corporate America" has ruined the main street economy by taking full advantage of the American worker and destroying the concept of "capitalism". "Corporate America" is fully responsible for ½ of the American people living in or near the poverty line and corporate America must – pay the price!

ABOUT THE AUTHOR

Terol, born in Virginia 10 days before the death of Franklin Delano Roosevelt, destined to become a political junkie. Drafted into the U.S. Military in 1965 and spent 16 months in Vietnam before being honorably discharged.

Very proud to have been a war veteran and have served in the military and proud as well of his father who served in the World War II and later on became President of the "Union" in which he served and dedicated his time trying to improve working conditions for his members.

He built his first business from scratch in 1963 and in a span of over 46 year's he owned, operated or supervised over 26 different businesses on "Main Street USA" that employed tens of thousands of workers.

Terol was a "hands on" owner and employer who worked side by side with his employees in an effort to create a positive work place where all his employees had respect for each other and the business they worked for.

He was one of the millions of entrepreneurs in this country that felt a duty to their community, their customers and their employees. He is proud to have been an entrepreneur in the United States of America and have served his country in the U.S. Military.

www.ingramcontent.com/pod-product-compliance
Lightning Source LLC
Chambersburg PA
CBHW030853180526
45163CB00004B/1553